IMAGES
of America

CYCLING IN CHICAGO

D1567171

Michigan Avenue, 1895

Riders on Michigan Avenue are portrayed in this illustration as they pass the Art Institute of Chicago in 1895. (Author's collection.)

IMAGES
of America

CYCLING IN
CHICAGO

Chris McAuliffe

ARCADIA
PUBLISHING

Published by Arcadia Publishing
Charleston, South Carolina

Printed in the United States of America

Library of Congress Control Number: 2017935892

For all general information, please contact Arcadia Publishing:
Telephone 843-853-2070
Fax 843-853-0044
E-mail sales@arcadiapublishing.com
For customer service and orders:
Toll-Free 1-888-313-2665

Visit us on the Internet at www.arcadiapublishing.com

To my wonderful wife, Mina, and my best buddy, Sabina our dog.

Contents

FOREWORD

For generations, Chicago has been on the forefront of the bicycling revolution. A flat landscape, a gridded street layout, and a breathtaking shoreline all invite people to get around on two wheels. It is a city that served, for a time, as the heart of the US bicycle manufacturing industry. And thanks to an abundance of local rail lines, Chicagoland was one of the first regions in the nation to start converting abandoned railroad lines into multiuse trails.

In recent decades, cycling has been regaining the standing it once had in Chicago. Since it was founded as the Chicagoland Bicycling Federation in 1985, the Active Transportation Alliance has been playing a key part in the local bicycling renaissance. A vibrant local bicycling community allowed cycling to shake off its reputation as a fringe activity and has become a mainstream mode of transportation that has allowed a huge number of residents to benefit from the power of the pedal. Since 2000, the number of people biking in the city has tripled, with an average of 125,000 bike trips taking place each day—and that is a conservative estimate. Bike riders throughout the region saw their travel options grow exponentially when the multiyear efforts of Active Trans, Metra, and more recently the South Shore Line began allowing bikes on board.

Chicago residents should be proud of the commitment and investment the City of Chicago has made to promote bicycling and improve its cycling infrastructure. The city has built more than 100 miles of buffered and protected bike lanes since 2011. The increase in bike lanes and ridership has been a boon to Divvy, the city's popular bike-share program that launched in 2013. With more than 580 stations and 5,800 bikes available in the city, Evanston, and Oak Park, Divvy has provided more than 10 million rides and has become the second-largest bike-share system in the United States.

Chicago's parks and trails are also a hit with people who ride bikes. The 606, an elevated trail and park system that runs through four neighborhoods on the northwest side, opened in June 2015 to much acclaim. Cyclists also hail Big Marsh Bike Park, which opened in November 2016 on the far southeast side. Once an industrial site, Big Marsh is the largest bike park in the Midwest. Due in large part to the efforts of Active Trans, the busiest trail in the nation, the Chicago Lakefront Trail, soon will be seeing a couple of key improvements: the completion of the Navy Pier Flyover and the creation of separate trails for people walking and biking along the trail's entirety.

All of these achievements helped Chicago grab the No. 1 spot in 2016 on *Bicycling* magazine's annual ranking of the 50 Best Bike Cities. While Chicago has emerged as a national leader in bicycling, it is important to keep in mind that few of these advances would have happened without a local group like Active Trans mobilizing people and demanding better options for getting around. While there have been plenty of successes, there is still much work to do so that more people feel safe and comfortable hopping on their bikes regularly to get to work, run errands, and get to school. Active Trans will remain on the front lines of improving local biking options by working with residents, decision makers, and other stakeholders to ensure cycling is easy and safe for everyone in the region.

—Ron Burke
Executive Director
Active Transportation Alliance, activetrans.org/join

ACKNOWLEDGMENTS

I am very grateful to the many people and organizations that provided materials and support for this book, like Oscar Wastyn Jr. and his son Scott Wastyn. The Wastyns gave me access to their tremendous archive of cycling photographs, newspaper clippings, and memorabilia. The Wastyn family has owned and operated Chicago's Oscar Wastyn Cycles for over 100 years.

Thank-yous go to Ron Burke and Ted Villaire of the Active Transportation Alliance for sharing their photographs and providing the preface of the book; Jeff Ruetsche of Arcadia Publishing for his patience; the US Bicycling Hall of Fame in Davis, California; Ben Helphand at the Friends of the Bloomingdale Trail; Randy Neufeld of SRAM for his early advice, insight, and guidance; the Kozy family; Turin Bicycles; Heritage Bicycles; the South Chicago Wheelmen; Steve Buchtel of Trails for Illinois; and Julia Bachrach at the Chicago Park District.

Thanks also go to the George Garner family for providing photographs of George Garner Cyclery, North Central College for allowing me access to its tremendous Illinois Prairie Path archives, Suzie LaBelle of the Evanston Bike Club, John Kline of the Kenosha Velodrome, Joe Beemster of the Wheeling Wheelmen, Tracy Dangott of XXX Racing-Athletico, Richard Schwinn of Waterford Bikes (thanks for the factory tour!), Sharon Budde for her great suggestions and advice, and finally my wife, Mina, for her support and patience.

Images without a parenthetical credit line are from the author's collection.

INTRODUCTION

Chicago has a rich and diverse bicycling history. In the late 19th and early 20th centuries, Chicago was the center of bicycle manufacturing in the United States. As the industry evolved from the early velocipedes or high wheelers, which had one huge wheel in the front and no brakes, to the more modern safety bike, Chicago grew as a hub of activity. As an early industrial and transportation center, Chicago was ideal for bicycle manufacturers. According to the 1898 *Chicago Bicycle Directory: A Reference Book of the Trade*, approximately two-thirds of the country's bicycles and accessories were manufactured within 150 miles of the city; Chicago was the Detroit of bike manufacturing. Chicago's Lake Street was known as Bicycle Row due to the concentration of bicycle factories.

Manufacturers such as the Mead Cycle Company, Gormully & Jeffrey, Monarch Bicycles, Western Wheels Works, and Arnold, Schwinn & Company manufactured hundreds of thousands of bicycles each year. In 1895, the industry sold over 800,000 bicycles. By 1897, that number reached 2 million. By the late 1890s, due to increased competition and sharp decreases in manufacturing costs, the average cost of a bicycle dropped below $100. Bicycles were sold not just in bicycles stores, but also in hardware, department, drug, and clothing stores. Downward pressure on pricing continued as manufacturers fought for market share, driving prices even lower. By 1899, the bicycle boom turned into a bust as the industry experienced a glut of inventory in the marketplace, combined with the rise of the horseless carriage (automobile). By 1905, national bicycle sales were 25 percent of what they were in 1900.

One company prospered were many others failed. Arnold, Schwinn & Company saw an opportunity and purchased many failing competitors at rock-bottom prices. In addition, Schwinn built a state of the art factory on Chicago's west side. Sears, Roebuck and Co. built its massive merchandise distribution facility in the city's Homan Square neighborhood. Completed in 1906, it served as the national distribution point for the thousands of Sears, Roebuck and Co. products, including its popular Elgin bicycle brand.

For decades, Chicago was also a center of track and road racing. Six-day races drew capacity crowds at the Chicago Stadium, Chicago Coliseum, and International Amphitheatre. In 1893, A.A. Zimmerman, one of the world's greatest cycling sprint riders, won the first International Cycling Association world championship, held in conjunction with the World's Columbian Exposition in Chicago. Marshall "Major" Taylor set his first world record for the fastest one-mile race, in 1899, on the Garfield Park Velodrome. Taylor, also known as "The Black Cyclone," got his start racing on Chicago's cycling tracks before going on to become the world sprint champion in 1899 and 1900. Taylor was African American and had to compete in northern states and in Europe because he was barred from competition in the South.

The Chicago Coliseum and International Amphitheatre hosted velodrome races through the mid-1950s. The Chicago Stadium, built as the permanent home for the Chicago Blackhawks, hosted 6-day races that matched or surpassed the hockey games in attendance. Racers such as Carl Stockholm, Edwin Pesak, Bobby Walthour Jr., Freddie Spencer, and many other professional racers all gained fame and wealth racing on the 6-day race circuit. Chicago bike racers also competed at Sherman Park, the Humboldt Park Velodrome, and on Chicago's famed Magnificent Mile in road and track competitions.

In the 1930s, the bike industry experienced a resurgence in quality and design after a period of low quality and a lack of innovation. During the 1920s, the industry was flooded by cheap inferior-quality bicycles that were sold in department and hardware stores instead of bicycle shops. In 1933, Frank Schwinn wanted to improve the quality of bicycles and developed a heavy-framed bicycle with more durable "balloon tires." The balloon tire bicycle, actually named the B-10E, revolutionized the industry and helped keep the Schwinn factory on Kildare Avenue busy with orders during the height of the Depression.

Also in 1933, the Century of Progress Exposition (world's fair) took place on Chicago's lakefront. The exposition represented an opportunity for the industrial world to show off its newest innovations, including advances in the bicycle industry. The bicycle exhibit featured early velocipedes to modern bikes. The exhibit helped showcase the progress made in the bicycle industry. The industry responded to the enthusiasm generated by the exposition by developing even more balloon cruiser bicycles, such as the Shelby Airflo, Schwinn Autocycle, and Schwinn Hollywood.

In the 1950s, Chicago was one of the first major cities to establish a network of bicycle paths through the city's parks and county's forest preserves. In 1959, Chicago hosted the third Pan American Games (similar to the Olympic Games). The track cycling events were held at the Gately Park Velodrome on the city's south side, while the road race was held on Lake Shore Drive.

Today, Chicago is a hub for recreational cyclists. Hundreds of miles of bike lanes; rails to trails bike paths such as the Illinois Prairie Path, the Bloomingdale Trail, and Lakefront Path; and the Big Marsh provide cyclists with numerous recreational and commuting options in a crowded urban environment. Chicago has elected several mayors who have made great contributions to the cycling culture of the city. Mayor Carter H. Harrison II campaigned with posters declaring that he was "Not the Champion Cyclist; But the Cyclists' Champion." Harrison won the mayoral election in part due to strong support from cyclists. Mayor Richard J. Daley, like Carter Harrison II, was a supporter of bicycling. During his administration, the city built a network of lakefront bicycle paths. His son Mayor Richard M. Daley continued on as a supporter of bicycling. His administration created nearly 100 miles of bike lanes, supported bike-friendly events like Bike the Drive and the LATE Ride, and initiated the Divvy bike-sharing program.

Mayor Rahm Emmanuel's administration has continued the work by constructing over 50 additional miles of protected bike lanes. Those lanes, and the Loop Link transit project, will enable Chicago to become the first major city in the nation to have a downtown network of protected bike lanes. In addition, the Bloomingdale Trail (also called the 606), an urban rails to trails bike path, opened in the spring of 2015 on the city's north side. The Big Marsh Bike Park, built on 278 acres of environmentally distressed land on the city's southeast side, features a BMX park, cyclo-cross course, multipurpose trails, and restored natural wetlands. The Navy Pier Flyover is an elevated path designed to improve walking and biking along the Lakefront Trail near Navy Pier—one of the most heavily used portions of the 18.5-mile trail. All of these projects contributed to *Bicycling* magazine naming Chicago as the "Best Bike City" of 2016.

This book provides readers with an entertaining and educational look at the fascinating history of cycling in Chicago. Readers will learn about the many colorful personalities, venues, and businesses that have all contributed to the diverse culture and history of cycling in Chicago.

One

THE EARLY DAYS

By the end of the 19th century, Chicago was the bicycle manufacturing capital of the United States. More than two-thirds of all bikes manufactured in the United States were made in Chicago. What Detroit was to auto manufacturing, Chicago was to bike manufacturing. Chicago was the ideal location for the industry. It already had over 2,000 miles of paved roads. The city had a thriving industrial and manufacturing base. Chicago's central location in the nation gave it remarkable access to markets via the nation's ever-expanding railroad network. Finally, Chicago had a can-do, entrepreneurial spirit that carried over from rebuilding of the city following the Great Chicago Fire of 1871. In short, Chicago was a tremendous industrial hub, ideal for manufacturing and distribution.

Over 90 bicycle manufacturers were located in the city, companies like Western Wheel Works, Century Cycle Manufacturing, James Cycle Company, Sterling Cycle Works, and Arnold, Schwinn & Company. Chicago even had "Bicycle Row" on West Lake Street, where many of the largest bicycle manufacturers were located. Many changes in production (a shift towards mass production) and design (lighter, more maneuverable bikes) helped fuel the dramatic increase in bike manufacturing. In the 1870s, a high wheel or velocipede bicycle could cost $300. By the late 1890s, the cost of an entry-level bicycle cost was around $35. In short, bicycling was transformed from a high-class pursuit to a sport open to the working class. Cycling clubs sprang up throughout the city, and cyclists became a political and economic force to be reckoned with.

Many great personal stories are associated with the early years of the bicycling industry and culture. Marshall "Major" Taylor was the first African American to win a world championship in cycling. In 1895, Annie "Londonderry" Kopchovsky was the first woman to ride a bicycle around the world. She did it on a Chicago-made Sterling brand bicycle.

Finally, in 1890, Ignaz Schwinn immigrated to the United States. By 1895, he partnered with meatpacker Arnold Adolph and incorporated Arnold, Schwinn & Company. Later known as the Schwinn Bicycle Company, it produced some of the most popular bicycles in history and dominated the industry well into the late 20th century.

Members of the Illinois Cycling Club stand outside their clubhouse on Chicago's west side around 1890. The club boasted a membership of over 1,000 cyclists. (Courtesy of Oscar Wastyn Archives.)

In 1899, the American Bicycle Company absorbed hundreds of bicycle manufacturers into a new "bicycle trust." Independent companies such as Monarch and Barnes became subsidiaries of the trust. Founded by Alfred Pope, it stifled competition and innovation. The trust was a financial failure—it defaulted on its corporate bonds in 1903 and ceased existence as a business entity.

Arthur Augustus Zimmerman was one of the world's greatest cycling sprint riders and winner of the first world championship in 1893. Known as "Zimmy," he was an American national champion in 1890, 1891, and 1892. In 1893, he won the International Cycling Association (ICA) world sprint and 10K championships held in Chicago. The first world championships were awarded to the United States, which hosted them in Chicago to coincide with the 1893 World's Columbian Exposition being held there. Zimmerman dominated the championships, winning two of the three gold medals awarded.

The Lakeview Cycling Club is shown in front of its clubhouse in the 1890s. Cycling clubs were common at the beginning of the 20th century. By the late 1890s, Chicago had 54 cycling clubs with a combined membership of over 10,000. (Courtesy of the *Chicago Tribune*.)

Racers J.E. Gill (left), C.A. Linde (center), and Ed Bukowski (right) line up to race their bicycles on North Michigan Avenue in Chicago in 1901. (Courtesy of the Library of Congress.)

Spectators watch a race in Chicago's Englewood neighborhood around 1897. Sherman Park, located in the Englewood neighborhood, was designed by renowned landscape architects John Charles Olmsted and Frederick Law Olmsted Jr. along with Chicago architect Daniel Burnham. It opened in 1905 and has hosted numerous road racing/criterium races over the years. (Courtesy of the *Chicago Tribune*.)

Elgin was the house brand of Chicago-based Sears, Roebuck and Co. The Elgin Motor-Bike was one of the models distributed and sold by Sears. From Sears' massive Homan Square warehouse, bicycles (and thousands of other consumer goods) were shipped by rail throughout the United States. The Elgin Bluebird, Cardinal, and Motor-bike were among the best sellers. (Courtesy of the North Homan Foundation Archives.)

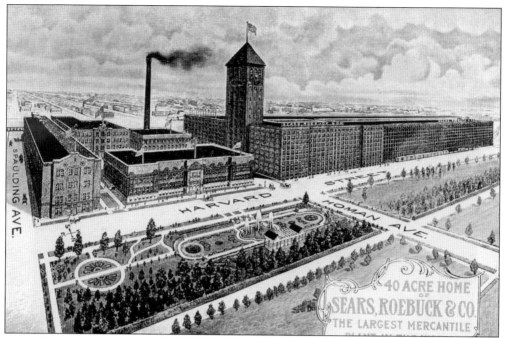

Founded in 1893, Sears, Roebuck and Co. was, by 1900, the country's largest mail-order company. In 1904, Sears purchased 41 acres in the Homan Square neighborhood for a massive central mail-order complex. Over 7,000 construction workers were hired to help build the facility. Each construction day, over 60 freight cars of materials were used to build the complex. The plant was finished in October 1906. (Courtesy of the North Homan Foundation Archives.)

Mail carriers at the Ravenswood Post Office stand with their mail delivery bicycles in 1894. (Courtesy of the Chicago Public Library.)

An advertisement for the Monarch Model No. 10 is shown here. Note the relatively lightweight bike—22 pounds. However, the $100 price would be equivalent to $2,857 in 2017 dollars. John William Kiser, a capitalist and manufacturer, founded the Monarch Cycle Manufacturing Company in 1892 with $500,000 in capital. At its peak, Monarch employed 300–400 engineers at its factory located at the corner of North Halsted and West Lake Streets in Chicago. (Courtesy of Oscar Wastyn Archives.)

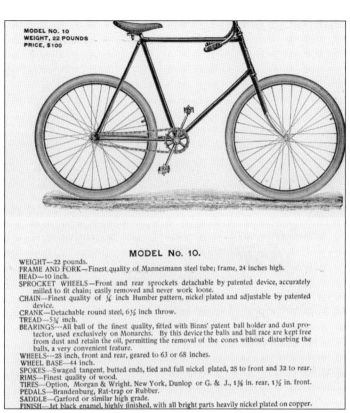

MODEL NO. 10
WEIGHT, 22 POUNDS
PRICE, $100

MODEL No. 10.

WEIGHT—22 pounds.
FRAME AND FORK—Finest quality of Mannesmann steel tube; frame, 24 inches high.
HEAD—10 inch.
SPROCKET WHEELS—Front and rear sprockets detachable by patented device, accurately milled to fit chain; easily removed and never work loose.
CHAIN—Finest quality of ¼ inch Humber pattern, nickel plated and adjustable by patented device.
CRANK—Detachable round steel, 6½ inch throw.
TREAD—5¾ inch.
BEARINGS—All ball of the finest quality, fitted with Binns' patent ball holder and dust protector, used exclusively on Monarchs. By this device the balls and ball race are kept free from dust and retain the oil, permitting the removal of the cones without disturbing the balls, a very convenient feature.
WHEELS—28 inch, front and rear, geared to 63 or 68 inches.
WHEEL BASE—44 inch.
SPOKES—Swaged tangent, butted ends, tied and full nickel plated, 28 to front and 32 to rear.
RIMS—Finest quality of wood.
TIRES—Option, Morgan & Wright, New York, Dunlop or G. & J., 1⅝ in. rear, 1¾ in. front.
PEDALS—Brandenburg, Rat-trap or Rubber.
SADDLE—Garford or similar high grade.
FINISH—Jet black enamel, highly finished, with all bright parts heavily nickel plated on copper.

❧ It Moves in Good Society ❧

THE $100 RAMBLER BICYCLE

A Model of Strength, Beauty, and Simplicity.
Beautiful book of details free.

GORMULLY & JEFFERY MFG. CO., Chicago.

Rambler Bicycle Agencies all over the U. S.

Gormully and Jeffrey was a large bicycle manufacturer in the 1890s. The company moved to Kenosha, Wisconsin, in 1900 to manufacturer automobiles. (Courtesy of Oscar Wastyn Archives.)

"Not a Champion Cyclist, but the Cyclist's Champion" was Chicago mayor Carter Harrison's slogan in his first campaign for mayor in 1897. (Courtesy of Oscar Wastyn Archives.)

John Mason prepares to ride his high wheeler bicycle in Garfield Park in 1885. (Courtesy of the Library of Congress.)

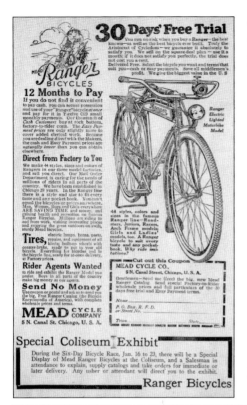

The Mead Ranger was produced by Mead Cycle Company from its factory located at 5 Canal Street in Chicago. It was among the city's first bicycle manufacturers, beginning operations in 1889. (Courtesy of the Library of Congress.)

Mead Cycle Factory sat across the street from the Chicago & North Western Railroad station around 1908. Mead was famous for the Ranger and Pathfinder bicycles. (Courtesy of the Library of Congress.)

George T. Robie founded the Excelsior Supply Company in Chicago in 1876. The company was a distributor of sewing machine parts. During the 1880s, as the popularity of the bicycle grew, the company branched out into cycle parts, supplies, and accessories. Excelsior became a major manufacturer of bicycles and bicycle equipment in the United States. (Courtesy of Oscar Wastyn Archives.)

George Robie's son Frederick was interested in manufacturing motorcycles and motorcars. In 1907, the company debuted its newly designed single-cylinder motorcycle— the Excelsior. The new motorcycle sold so well, the company had trouble keeping up with customer orders. (Courtesy of Oscar Wastyn Archives.)

After the success of the new motorcycle, Frederick Robie contacted architect Frank Lloyd Wright to design a house for his family. Construction began in 1909, and the house was completed in 1910. While the Robie family only lived in the house for about two years, it is still known as the Robie House—one of Chicago's most famous Frank Lloyd Wright homes. Today, the Frederick C. Robie House is a National Historic Landmark on the campus of the University of Chicago in the Hyde Park neighborhood of Chicago. (Courtesy of the *Chicago Tribune*.)

F.W. Schwinn is seen riding an Excelsior motorcycle. In 1912, Ignaz Schwinn bought the Excelsior Supply Company but had no interest in the bicycle division due to the success of his own Arnold, Schwinn & Company; Schwinn only bought the assets and name. After the purchase, there were two Excelsior names and companies that existed in Chicago. In 1916, the Excelsior Cycle Company moved from Chicago to Michigan City, Indiana. The Excelsior Motor & Manufacturing Company manufactured motorcycles (under the Excelsior brand) as part of Schwinn, until the company ceased operations in September 1931 due to the Depression. (Courtesy of Oscar Wastyn Archives.)

In 1895, Annie Kopchovsky, known as Annie Londonderry, was the first woman to bicycle around the world. Sterling Cycle Works of Chicago sponsored her trip and gave her a men's Expert Model E Light Roadster for the journey. (Courtesy of Oscar Wastyn Archives.)

Londonderry left Chicago on September 24, 1894, and returned on September 12, 1895, collecting the $10,000 prize. When she published an account of her adventure, a *New York World* headline described the trip as "The Most Extraordinary Journey Ever Undertaken by a Woman." (Courtesy of Oscar Wastyn Archives.)

Marshall Walter "Major" Taylor (November 26, 1878—June 21, 1932) won the world one-mile track cycling championship in 1899 after setting numerous world records. Taylor was the first African American cyclist to achieve the level of national and world champion. After retiring in 1908, Taylor fell on hard times and lost the fortune he amassed during his racing career. (Courtesy of the *Chicago Tribune*.)

After a stint of racing in Europe, Major Taylor (middle) prepares to race against Iver Lawson (left) and Willie Fenn in Massachusetts in 1899. (Courtesy of the US Bicycling Hall of Fame.)

Emil Wastyn (behind counter) poses in the original Wastyn Cycle Shop around 1916. In 1910, the Belgian bicycle builder immigrated to the United States. Wastyn opened a bicycle shop on Fullerton Avenue in Chicago and began a cycling dynasty that would last more than 100 years. He was the designer and builder of the original Schwinn Paramount in 1937. (Courtesy of Oscar Wastyn Archives.)

Al Flath (left) and Arnold Langher are training on a tandem racing bicycle in 1905 near Chicago. Flath was an endurance rider who held many national and local cycling records. He went on to become an official timer in the sports of speed skating and cycling for 70 years. Flath was inducted into the National Speedskating Hall of Fame in 1966. (Courtesy of Oscar Wastyn Archives.)

Al Flath takes a break from a training ride at Half Day, Illinois (now Vernon Hills, Illinois), in 1905. Flath and Arnold Langher were riding the traditional Milwaukee Avenue century training loop from Chicago to the northern suburbs (then just farm communities) and back. (Courtesy of Oscar Wastyn Archives.)

The *Chicago Inter Ocean* magazine portrayed bicycling as a pastime of the rich. This scene is from Lincoln Park near the U.S. Grant statute in 1893. *Chicago Inter Ocean* appealed to an active, upscale, and status-conscious readership. (Courtesy of Oscar Wastyn Archives.)

Defiance Bicycles was a Chicago-based bicycle manufacturer. Its marketing campaign also portrayed bicycling as the sport of upper-class men and women. (Courtesy of Oscar Wastyn Archives.)

The Garfield Park Velodrome is pictured in the early 1900s. Marshall "Major" Taylor set his first world record for the fastest one-mile race on this track in 1899. (Courtesy of Oscar Wastyn Archives.)

The Schwinn enameling department is seen here in 1916. Note the organized fashion of the frames and bright light. The factory on Kildare Avenue was a model of efficiency and order. (Courtesy of Oscar Wastyn Archives.)

By the early 20th century, the Schwinn factory was the standard for industrial efficiency and quality in the bicycle industry. (Courtesy of Oscar Wastyn Archives.)

The shipping department at the Schwinn factory is pictured here. Note the Arnold, Schwinn & Company World Cycles boxes. The trade name "World" was symbolic of the company's great ambitions in the early 20th century. (Courtesy of Oscar Wastyn Archives.)

Two

THE GLORY DAYS

In the early part of the 20th century, the sport of bicycling seemed to be fading. In 1900, over one million bicycles were produced. By 1904, that number dropped to 250,000. Following what was called the "Bicycle Bust," bicycling boomed again in the 1920s, as bicycles became more affordable and accessible. Bike racing quickly rose to become one of the most watched sports in America. Six-day races grew in popularity and were viewed by tens of thousands of fans at venues such as Madison Square Garden, the Cleveland Coliseum, and the Chicago Stadium. Velodromes popped up throughout the nation. Six-day cyclists were some of the highest-paid athletes of the era. As the nation grew, paved roads became commonplace, and bicycles were a cheap and efficient form of transportation.

Bicycle manufacturers began to focus more and more on appearance and comfort for the rider. Bicycles with shock absorbers, "spring forks," balloon tires, headlights, and frames resembling motorcycles soon began to emerge from the industry's factories. The frames were painted in bright glossy colors and featured chrome parts. All seemed to have classic streamlined designs.

Bicycling was a cheap and healthy form of recreation. Cycle trains left Chicago for weekend trips to the hinterlands in what is now suburbia. They allowed the urban rider a respite from the crowded and dirty streets of the city. The League of American Cyclists sponsored many train trips to and from major American cities. When World War II began, manufacturers, like Schwinn, quickly retooled their factories to produce war material. Since fuel was scarce for civilian use, bicycles were a cheap form of transportation. Balloon tire bicycles, once developed for the children's market, soon began to appear in the adolescent and adult markets. Between early 1930s and the late 1940s, bicycling was at the peak of its popularity.

Riding through the countryside became an important recreational and social activity for bicyclists, particularly during World War II, when fuel rationing discouraged the use of private automobiles. Here, a Chicago cycle train unloads its passengers. (Courtesy of Oscar Wastyn Archives.)

Chicago police officer John Berry issues a ticket to American rider Harry Horan, seated, and French rider Marcel Guimbretiere for "speeding" at Clark and Madison Streets on a Liberty Limited in February 1931. The two bicycle racers were in town for the 6-day bike race that started on February 8, 1931, at the Chicago Stadium. (Courtesy of the *Chicago Tribune*.)

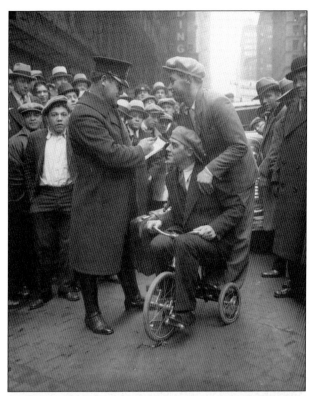

Eddie Trieste, a bike racer from the south side of Chicago, takes a spill during the 31st International Chicago 6-Day Bike Race, which started on March 11, 1934. "There were six spills during the first two hours of the race," the *Chicago Tribune* reported. "None of the thrills of bike racing was missing for the opening night's customers. The crowd of 10,500 was almost a record breaker." (Courtesy of Oscar Wastyn Archives.)

Bike racer Bill Jacoby was an amateur racer in the 1940s and a regular 6-day racer in the 1950s. Jacoby won many races at the Humboldt Park bicycle bowl during the 1940s. Jacoby's last race was in 1958. (Courtesy of the *Chicago Tribune*.)

Endurance bicyclists were all the rage in 1930, including Victor Preisinger, age 15, of 5009 South Artesian Avenue. The ice-cream cone he is eating was a gift from one of his young fans on July 16, 1930. (Courtesy of the *Chicago Tribune*.)

From left to right, Gilbert Livingston, Bradley Clarkson, Billy Sheahan (on bike), Bud Forbes, and Edwin Orr are pictured on July 23, 1930, in Chicago. (Courtesy of the *Chicago Tribune*.)

Ignaz Schwinn is pictured in his office on North Kilder Avenue with son Frank Schwinn in 1931. (Courtesy of Oscar Wastyn Archives.)

The Schwinn Racing Team lines up for a promotional photograph. In the 1930s, Schwinn sponsored a bicycle racing team headed by Emil Wastyn, who designed the team's bikes. The Schwinn team competed in 6-day racing across the United States with riders such as Jerry Rodman and Russell Allen. (Courtesy of Oscar Wastyn Archives.)

In 1938, Frank W. Schwinn officially introduced the Paramount series. Developed from experience gained in racing, Schwinn established Paramount as its answer to high-end, professional competition bicycles. The Paramount used high-strength chrome-molybdenum steel alloy tubing and expensive brass lug-brazed construction. (Courtesy of Oscar Wastyn Archives.)

During the next 20 years, most of the Paramount bikes would be built in limited numbers at a small frame shop headed by Wastyn, in spite of Schwinn's continued efforts to bring all-frame production into the factory. (Courtesy of Oscar Wastyn Archives.)

On May 17, 1941, Alfred Letourneur was able to beat the motor-paced world speed record on a bicycle, reaching 108.92 miles per hour (175.29 km/h) on a Schwinn Paramount bicycle riding behind a car in Bakersfield, California. (Courtesy of Oscar Wastyn Archives.)

Chicago mayor William Dever, right, is pictured with racer Carl Stockholm at the 6-day bicycle races that started on March 20, 1927, at the Dexter Park Pavilion. "Carl Stockholm, a Chicago boy and one of the most popular riders in the race, has a good opportunity to win the coming grind," the *Chicago Tribune* reported before the start of a 6-day race in 1927. Stockholm and Italian rider Franco Georgetti won the race. A decorated veteran of both world wars, Stockholm was an Olympic cyclist in 1920 and a popular 6-day bicycle race champion during the ensuing decade. (Courtesy of Oscar Wastyn Archives.)

Carl Stockholm grew up in Zion, Illinois. He joined the US Army at age 17 and served in France during World War I. He earned four battle stars and the Purple Heart. Wounded in the knee, Stockholm was told he might never walk again and was encouraged to repair the injury by bike riding. Eventually, he was able to qualify for the 1920 US Olympic team. Stockholm was the owner of Stockholm Cleaners, which at one time had two plants and a chain of 20 dry cleaners in the Chicago area. His Stockholm Cleaners was featured as the official cleaners of the 1933 Chicago World's Fair, the Century of Progress International Exposition, for which he designed a glass-enclosed, state-of-the-art cleaning plant. (Courtesy of Oscar Wastyn Archives.)

Proclaimed the world's youngest cyclist, Sherry Brenner leads fellow cyclists to the Chicago Park District offices in the mid-1930s to ask for more bike paths in Chicago's parks. (Courtesy of Sherry Brenner.)

Popular "cycle trains" took city riders to the country for weekend excursions. Here, a group rides near Barrington in the late 1940s. (Courtesy of Sherry Brenner.)

Bicycle Day at the 1934 Century of Progress International Exposition in Chicago brought out many cyclists. (Courtesy of Sherry Brenner.)

Two 6-day racers refuel after a day of endurance racing at the Chicago Stadium. The race participants consumed thousands of calories each race day to fuel their bodies for competition. (Courtesy of Oscar Wastyn Archives.)

WHAT THE RIDERS EAT—

To begin with, six chefs are busy in the kitchen for the 144 hours of the race, preparing food for them. They are under the supervision of Jack Neville, who for twenty-five years has devoted his life to the training of bike racers; and of Charley Stein, the steward.

Here is the meat order that went into the Garden for the race. Twelve sides of beef, out of which will be carved 500 juicy steaks, 400 chickens, 600 pounds of lamb chops, ten boiled hams, and fifty pounds of bacon. Lamb is the favorite meat of the riders, but when they get a chance to eat something more substantial they take a steak or half a chicken.

All the riders eat a lot of vegetables during the race. Here is the list of what the vegetable man had to carry into the Garden: Three barrels of potatoes, four baskets of string beans, four barrels of spinach, ten dozen cans of asparagus, eight cases of peas, 100 bunches of celery, two bushels of onions, 200 heads of lettuce, 50 quarts of tomatoes, and twenty-five heads of cabbage.

During the week in the line of fruits the following will be consumed: Seventy pounds of prunes, two barrels of apples for apple sauce, six boxes of eating apples, 1,000 oranges, 300 grapefruit and twelve dozen lemons.

Three hundred dozen eggs are consumed during the week. The riders eat a great deal of custard made from eggs. The order for milk is 700 quarts for the week, while the riders eat fifty pounds of butter. The chief beverage is coffee, and the week's supply is seventy-five pounds, while there is twenty pounds of tea consumed and five pounds of cocoa. In the cereal line the riders eat fifty pounds of rice, twenty pounds of oatmeal, six dozen boxes of cornflakes and also use 250 pounds of sugar.

Charley Stein has to look out for all the wants of the riders, which include thirty toothbrushes, thirty eye cups, thirty nose and throat atomizers, twenty-five gallons of rub-down, thirty combs and brushes, 500 Turkish towels, fifty mattresses, covers, and pillows.

All diets prescribed by Dr. E. Thomas Brand. He kept the riders in trim, setting bones, healing cuts. They may be down but they're never out, says Dr. Brand.

RULES FOR SCORING POINTS

THREE SERIES OF SPRINTS DAILY

Ten Sprints at 2:00 a. m. Ten at 3:00 p. m. Ten at 9:30 p. m. Distance of each sprint to be two miles.
Scoring of Points for each Sprint (except Saturday) will count as follows:

6 Points to Winning Team	2 Points to Third Team
4 Points to Second Team	1 Point to Fourth Team

On Saturday morning and afternoon the series of ten sprints will be conducted at the same time, but the scoring will be changed to 12 points for winning teams, while 2d, 3d and 4th positions of each sprint will remain the same as other days.

In event of any team gaining a lap on the field during any part of the race, including the last hour, said team shall retain its position as leader in the race, as long as the team holds its position as leader, but in the scoring of points any such team in lead on mileage shall be credited only with such points as it may win in the sprints, irrespective of the fact that the team may be a lap in the lead. Where two or more teams are tied in mileage, their final position in race is determined by the number of points won by them during the week's sprints.

FINAL SPRINTS—LAST HUOR OF RACE

On Saturday night there will be a Sprint Every Mile to the Finish for one hour. The Final Hour Sprints will start at 10 p. m. and finish at 11 p. m.

All points scored during the week will be added to points scored in final hour of race.

FINAL HOUR SCORING—During the last hour the points will score as follows:

72 Points to Winner of Each Sprint	2 Points to Third Team
4 Points to Second Team	1 Point to Fourth Team

RULES

The contestants in the race are not the only ones governed by stringent rules and regulations. All concessionaires also are required to observe rules.

Mr. Harmon's chief rule is that a ten-cent cigar shall sell for 10 cents and not for 15 cents. This applies to cigarettes, bottled goods, candies, sandwiches, in fact, everything sold here. All concessions handled by the management.

Any deviation from these popular prices should be reported immediately at the office.

P. T. ("PADDY") HARMON

5982 Seats at 50c for Circus and 101 Ranch
Chicago Stadium, March 30

This "What the Riders Eat" advertisement is from the *Chicago Stadium Review.* Note the heavy focus on meat, potatoes, vegetables, and coffee. (Courtesy of Oscar Wastyn Archives.)

F.W. Schwinn (center) is pictured with sons Edward Sr. (left) and Frank V. (right) in the late 1940s. (Courtesy of Oscar Wastyn Archives.)

F.W. Schwinn receives the American Defense Service Medal for service to the American war effort; Ignaz Schwinn looks on. In 1942, Schwinn ceased commercial bicycle production altogether (though the military ordered some 10,000 bicycles per year) to focus on military machinery production. (Courtesy of Oscar Wastyn Archives.)

Workers are in the brazing room during World War II producing airborne radar units. During the war, Schwinn shifted virtually all production to war-related materials. Women made up the majority of production-line workers during the war. (Courtesy of Oscar Wastyn Archives.)

The 1948 United States Olympic Cycling Team is en route to London aboard the SS *America*. The team included Chicagoan Al Stiller. Stiller started racing in the late 1930s but saw his career interrupted by World War II. Following the war, he competed in the 1947 World Cycling Championships and the 1948 London Olympics. He competed in the men's team pursuit and men's tandem sprint. After retiring from cycling, Stiller ran a bike shop in Chicago from 1960 to 1980. (Courtesy of Oscar Wastyn Archives.)

Round and 'round they go

Who's doing what?

Are riders pedaling bik
are bikes pedaling ri
That's question as ve
bicycle jockeys work o
Grant park for 46th Int
tional six-day bike
Event starts Oct. 11 at
seum, with several fo
stars being imported to
against best in U. S. Qu
(at left) spinning w h
while on their backs are
known to Chicago fans.
are (l. to r.) Jules Audy
win Pesek, Charley Ya
and Bill Jacoby.
TIMES Photos by John Zing

Jules Audy, Erwin Pesek, Charlie Yaccino, and Bill Jacoby pedal upside down in Chicago's Grant Park for a *Chicago Daily Times* story promoting the upcoming 46th International 6-Day Bike Race at the Chicago Coliseum. In 6-day races, one partner would ride while the other slept or ate. Shifts lasted several hours. (Courtesy of the *Chicago Daily Times* Archives.)

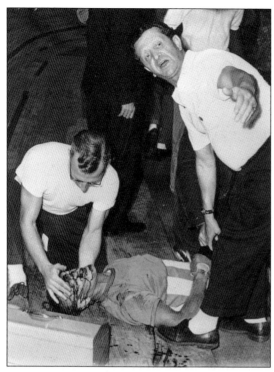

Cycling on a velodrome can be extremely dangerous, as this photograph shows. Ed Pesek crashed to the wood track at full speed (40-plus miles per hour) during a race at the International Amphitheatre. He suffered a serious head injury. Helmets were rarely worn back then, and there were no regulations requiring the use of protective headgear. (Courtesy of Oscar Wastyn Archives.)

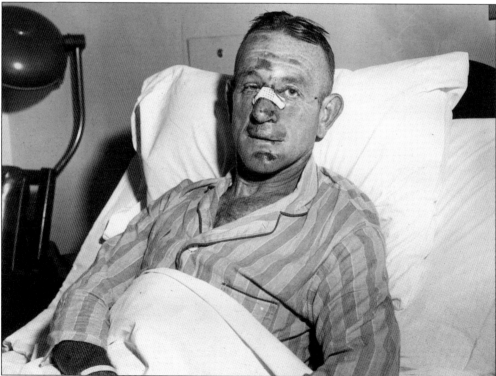

Ed Pesek is seen here a few days after the crash recovering in a Chicago hospital. Following a period of recovery, Pesek resumed track and road racing. (Courtesy of Oscar Wastyn Archives.)

Erwin Pesak kids around with Torchy Pedan in Chicago's Grant Park. The article was for an upcoming race at the Chicago Coliseum. (Courtesy of Oscar Wastyn Archives.)

LET'S JUST START ALL OVER

Erwin Pesek has a bit of fun with Torchy Peden, veteran six da bike rider, by holding back the latter's wheel as the pair worked ou with other riders in Grant park yesterday. These riders will con in the six day race which opens in the Coliseum April 28.

READY FOR THE LONG GRIND

A star field is ready to begin the six day bike race which opens tonight in the Coliseum. T oup of riders, eager to start in Chicago's first post-war cycle marathon, is looking forward to ent with keen anticipation. Left to right, Cocky O'Brien, Charley Logan, Val Melchiori, T etta and Cesare Moretti.

From left to right, Cocky O'Brien, Charley Logan, Val Melchiori, Tom Saetta, and Cesare Moretti prepare for the first 6-day race held after World War II. The venue was the familiar Chicago Coliseum. (Courtesy of Oscar Wastyn Archives.)

JACOBY - RICHTER , HIGHLAND PK.

Bill Jacoby (left) and Heinz Richter carry their bikes up a sand dune in north suburban Highland Park. Today, the ride from Chicago to Highland Park and back remains a popular training ride for cyclists of all abilities. (Courtesy of Oscar Wastyn Archives.)

Oscar Wastyn Jr. (at age 5) and his cousin Joanie Lammens are pictured in Lincoln Park in 1936. (Courtesy of Oscar Wastyn Archives.)

The League of American Bicyclists and the American Youth Hostels formed a joint program to run "cycle trains" that allowed city dwellers to travel to various locations for organized bike trips. Here, a group from Chicago poses for a photograph at the Decatur, Illinois, train station in the early 1940s. (Courtesy of Oscar Wastyn Archives.)

The League of American Bicyclists group from Chicago took a long trip to the Ozarks in 1941. (Courtesy of Oscar Wastyn Archives.)

Three

HISTORIC RACES AND RIDES

As popularity grew, so did the number of professional and amateur races, along with organized, recreational rides. For example, the annual Chicago Road Race traveled from Wheeling (then a tiny farming community) to downtown Chicago. Thousands watched the race as it approached the finish line at Jackson and Michigan Avenues. The Elgin-to-Chicago bicycle race was popular in the 1930s and 1940s and continued into the mid-1960s. The Chicago Stadium, Chicago Coliseum, and International Amphitheatre hosted international 6-day races for several decades. Outdoor velodromes in Humboldt Park and Garfield Park hosted top professional and weekly amateur races.

In addition, Chicago has played host to numerous track, road, and cyclo-cross national championships. In 1959, it hosted the Third Pan American Games (held every four years, one year prior to the upcoming Olympic Games). Over the last 125 years, Chicago has been the home of at least 12 different velodromes. Both Northbrook and Kenosha Velodromes have hosted Olympic trials and national championships.

Today, Chicago is ranked as one of the best bicycling cities in America. Events such as the LATE Ride, North Shore Century Ride, and Bike the Drive attract tens of thousands of bicycling enthusiasts to the lakefront each year. Bike the Drive alone attracts over 20,000 riders each year. These events serve as a reminder of the popularity of bicycling in the metropolitan area.

The Pullman Road Race, an annual Memorial Day event, started in front of the Leland Hotel at the intersection of Michigan Avenue and Van Buren Street. It attracted 200–300 racers, most from the city's numerous cycling clubs. (Courtesy of Keystone-Mast Collection, UCR/California Museum of Photography, University of California at Riverside.)

A large crowd of spectators gathers on May 30, 1893, just south of the brand-new Art Institute to watch the Pullman Road Race. The bicycle race from North Michigan Avenue to the Pullman neighborhood on the city's south side was the most popular cycling race of the year. (Courtesy of Keystone-Mast Collection, UCR/California Museum of Photography, University of California at Riverside.)

Pictured is the official program cover from the International 6-Day Team Bike Race held January 16–22, 1921, at the Chicago Coliseum. (Courtesy of Oscar Wastyn Archives.)

Shown is the official program cover for the 30th International 6-Day Bike Race held October 29–November 4, 1932, at the Chicago Stadium. (Courtesy of Oscar Wastyn Archives.)

Miss 6-Day Race, riders, and race officials pause before the start of the 47th International 6-Day Bike Race held at the International Amphitheatre. The race ran from October 31 to November 5, 1948. (Courtesy of Oscar Wastyn Archives.)

This is an interior page from the program for the 30th International 6-Day Bicycle Race. Six-day races remained popular throughout the 1930s. The Depression and the rise of the automobile contributed to the demise of the racing series. Between 1915 and 1957, fifty individual 6-day races were held in Chicago. (Courtesy of Oscar Wastyn Archives.)

These were the official rules of the
International 6-Day Team Bike Race.
(Courtesy of Oscar Wastyn Archives.)

NATIONAL CYCLING ASSOCIATION

Rules and Conditions Governing

Grand International Professional Six-Day Team Race

The race will start at 9 o'clock October 29th, and will finish at 12 P. M., November 4th. The contestants having the right to rest and ride as they may see fit, except that no rider must be on the track more than twelve hours in each twenty-four hours. The riders will be off the bicycle track between the hours of six and ten in the morning while the building is being cleaned, for sanitary reasons.

COLORS

Every team upon entering must select its colors, which must be worn at all times during the race, both in the racing shirt and in the sweater when one is worn.

The management insists that the regulations concerning the wearing of colors by competitors be strictly observed. Riders appearing without their original colors will be subject to a fine. Should a rider persist in appearing on the track without his proper colors he is liable to a forfeiture of all prize moneys.

RIDERS MUST REMAIN ON THE TRACK

It is imperative for the success of the race that the field shall be complete at all times, and in the interval between the bells announcing the resumption of the race, riders must not stop or dismount from their wheels, or ride on the floor, without the permission of the referee. Any rider dismounting without obtaining the consent of the referee will be penalized one lap.

A second offense will be deemed cause for disbarment from the race. Any rider who, in the judgment of the referee, allows himself to be deliberately lapped during the interval between the bells shall be fined for the offense.

REGARDING LAPS GAINED

1. Any lap or laps gained unfairly through one or more contestants sacrificing himself or themselves for one or more others shall not be allowed, and those implicated in such unfair riding must be disciplined for the race, and, in the judgment of the Board of Referees, may be reported to the N. C. A. Board of Control for further punishment.

2. In connection with the gaining of a lap by two or more riders, if it appears that they are assisted by one or more riders through holding back of others, no lap shall be allowed and all implicated shall be disciplined by the Board of Referees, and reported for further punishment to the N. C. A. Board of Control.

3. In case there is a doubt regarding the legality of a lap gained, a rider having a protest must file it with the Board of Referees in writing within an hour.

IN RELIEVING PARTNERS

In relieving his mate, a rider must mount in front of his cot on the stretch in which his camp is located, and start ahead of all other riders, and the relieved one must be positively on an equality with his mate before being considered out of the race. All pickups are to be made clean, and the rider making a pickup who does not wait for his partner to get alongside of him, will be penalized one lap. A group or groups of riders shall not follow any rider's wheel before they are in the race and relief has been made in a proper manner as prescribed above.

In relieving, the members of a team must not interfere with other contestants, and the relieved rider must hold the pole and not pass the score stand more than once after having been relieved. Furthermore, this relieved rider must make a positive stop on the stretch in front of his cot.

The second black line from the pole shall designate the highest part of the track that riders may use when not actually racing. Riders relieving their partners, or after being relieved must stay below the outer black line.

UNFAIR RIDING, ETC.

Contestants who are guilty of unfair riding, or who are ungentlemanly in dress, language, or conduct, may be disqualified by the referee at any part of the race, and upon such disqualification the contestant forfeits all rights to prizes, entrance fees, or any returns of prizes whatever, as provided for in this contract.

"Stalling" in every form shall be considered unfair riding, and any rider who makes a legitimate effort to get to the front from any part of the field must be given a fair share of the track on which to make his effort. Deliberate wide riding on the part of any one or more contestants will be considered sufficient cause for fines, and possible disqualifications.

Attention is called to the fact that a rider who is leading the field, or is in leading position at the time he is relieved by his partner, must leave the track on the pole or inside position, so as not to interfere with the field. Any departure from this rule will be considered unfair riding, and the rider shall be subject to fine and possible disqualification.

During a jam or sprint any rider that is losing a lap cannot be relieved except by the proper method prescribed by the rules. Should said rider's partner come on the track, and get into the field of leaders, without making the proper relief, the team shall be penalized one lap for each and every offense.

IN REFERENCE TO ACCIDENTS TO MACHINE

In case of a puncture or other accidents to his wheel, a rider must not be off the track more than ten laps, or else must be relieved by his teammate. The damaged wheel must be shown at once to the acting referee or his representative. One lap will be the penalty for any rider disobeying the above rule.

An accident in the form of a puncture, a broken handlebar, a broken chain, or a broken pedal, may, in the judgment of the Board of Referees, result in the loss of no laps in the score.

Harry Berz congratulates the winner of
a sprint race in August 1948. The 11-day
Cook County Fair was held at Chicago's
Soldier Field. Berz was a cycling and
speed skating race promoter, an Illinois
state representative, and a member of
the National Speedskating Hall of Fame.
(Courtesy of Oscar Wastyn Archives.)

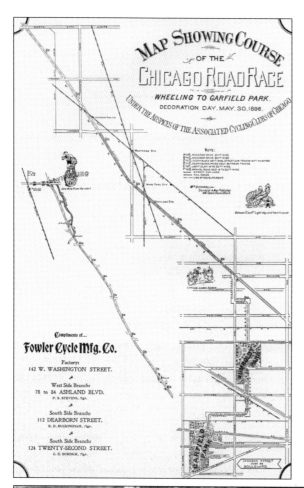

The Chicago Road Race began in Wheeling and ended in Chicago's Garfield Park on Decoration Day (now Memorial Day), May 30, 1896. (Courtesy of Oscar Wastyn Archives.)

Ted Smith, of Buffalo, New York; Tom Montemage, also of Buffalo; and Richard Olda, of St. Louis, finished first, second, and third, respectively, in the senior men's five-mile bicycle race at Humboldt Park on August 18, 1945. There was a spill in the race involving 12 cyclists, seven of whom received hospital treatment. Smith, 17, won the 17th National Amateur Bicycle Race held by the Amateur Bicycle League of America. (Courtesy of the *Chicago Tribune*.)

NATIONAL CHAMPIONSHIP CYCLO CROSS

AT THE PALOS PARK COURSE * * * * OCTOBER 20, 1963

* * * * * * CHICAGO, ILLINOIS * * * * * *

Sponsored By:

★

PRESIDENT
THEO KRON
248 W. 119th STREET

SOUTH CHICAGO
WHEELMEN

SECRETARY
MAC BOTTEMA
10960 S. PROSPECT AVE

The South Chicago Wheelmen hosted the 1st National Cyclocross Championship in Palos Park, Illinois (Palos Forest Preserve District). The South Chicago Wheelmen, organized in 1923, is one of the oldest bicycle racing teams in Illinois. Theo Kron, team president, was a leader in the Chicago cycling community for decades. (Courtesy of Oscar Wastyn Archives.)

Leroy "Tyger" Johnson of Rockford, Illinois, rests after the finish of the National Cyclocross Championship in Palos Park, Illinois, on October 12, 1969. Johnson worked at a dairy farmer in Rockford, Illinois, and won the first national cyclo-cross championship, held at Palos Park, Illinois, in 1963. Johnson went on to win two more national championships in 1966 and 1967. (Courtesy of Oscar Wastyn Archives.)

Pictured is the program cover from the 1963 National Bicycle Championships, held at the Northbrook Bicycle Track. Jim Rossi won 12 Illinois state championships and six national championships. He raced with two US teams in the 1956 Melbourne and 1960 Rome Olympics. He was also on two teams at the Pan American Games, competing in Chicago in 1959 and São Paulo, Brazil, in 1963. (Courtesy of Oscar Wastyn Archives.)

Shown is a program cover from the 1966 National Bicycle Championships, held at the Northbrook Bicycle Track (now Northbrook Velodrome) from August 19 to August 21, 1966. The Northbrook Velodrome has hosted numerous national, regional, and state championships since it opened in 1960. (Courtesy of Oscar Wastyn Archives.)

Bike the Drive is a non-competitive recreational bike ride held on the Sunday of Memorial Day weekend on Lake Shore Drive. The roadway is closed to motor vehicle traffic and open only to cyclists. The event benefits the Active Transportation Alliance. (Courtesy of Travis Roozee and the Active Transportation Alliance.)

Bike the Drive was launched in 2002 by the Chicago Bicycle Federation (predecessor to the Active Transportation Alliance). It was an immediate hit with Chicago bicycling enthusiasts. It draws more than 20,000 bicyclists each year and runs nearly the entire length of Lake Shore Drive—a total of 30 miles. (Courtesy of Travis Roozee and the Active Transportation Alliance.)

Bike the Drive riders take a break and admire the Chicago skyline near the bridge spanning the Chicago River. (Courtesy of Travis Roozee and the Active Transportation Alliance.)

Road racers leave the starting line for an early 1960s road race on the quiet, hilly roads surrounding the Palos Forest Preserve in Palos Park, Illinois. The Palos Forest Preserve, or simply Palos, is a destination for Chicago-area road, cyclo-cross, and mountain bike enthusiasts. Today, the area hosts the Illinois State Road Race and Mountain Bike Championships. (Courtesy of Oscar Wastyn Archives.)

The release of 5,000 doves into the air, heralds the oath of good sportsmanship in Soldier Field, Chicago, site of the 3rd Pan-American Games.

Opening ceremonies for the 1959 Pan American Games, held at Soldier Field in Chicago, are shown here. The games were very successful for the United States. The team won first place 120 times out of a possible 163 and picked up a total of 182 medals. In cycling, there were five medal events, with only men competing. The United States won one gold medal and two silver medals. (Courtesy of Oscar Wastyn Archives.)

In the Team Pursuit (4000m), the Argentinian men's pursuit team sets off from the starting line at the 1959 Pan American Games. A temporary velodrome was constructed at Gately Park on East 103rd Street on the south side of Chicago. (Courtesy of Oscar Wastyn Archives.)

Richard Cortright, of the US track cycling team, gets a massage during the track events at the Pan American Games. Cortright represented the United States at the 1952, 1956, and 1960 Olympics and won a gold medal in Team Pursuit (4000m) at the 1959 Pan American Games. (Courtesy of Oscar Wastyn Archives.)

In the Team Pursuit (4000m), the Uruguayan men's team celebrates its silver medal by taking a lap around the track. (Courtesy of Oscar Wastyn Archives.)

The US team takes a victory lap after winning the gold medal in the Team Pursuit Men (4,000m). The team consists of, from left to right, Jim Rossi, Robert Pfarr, Dick Cortright, and Charley Hewitt. (Courtesy of Oscar Wastyn Archives.)

The Argentinian team takes its spot on the third-place podium following the pursuit race. (Courtesy of Oscar Wastyn Archives.)

Gold, silver, and bronze medalists in the Team Pursuit Men (4000m) stand for the playing of the US national anthem, "The Star-Spangled Banner." (Courtesy of Oscar Wastyn Archives.)

Cook County board president Seymour Simon fires the starter's pistol at the 1964 Elgin-to-Chicago bicycle race. The race ran at various times between 1926 and 1964 on Route 31 and Route 14. (Courtesy of Oscar Wastyn Archives.)

The start of the Joliet-to-Chicago Bicycle Race, in the mid-1930s, is pictured in downtown Joliet. (Courtesy of Oscar Wastyn Archives.)

Racers ride past the famous Blackstone Hotel during the 1978 Chicago Tribune Boul Mich Bike Rally on September 16, 1979. Over 200 racers competed in three separate races. The one-mile course took riders along Michigan Avenue, Balbo Drive, Jackson Drive, Columbus Drive, and Jackson Boulevard. (Courtesy of Oscar Wastyn Archives.)

Chicago Tribune Boul Mich Bike Rally racers ride past Buckingham Fountain during the 1978 road race. The race, sponsored by the *Chicago Tribune* and the Michigan Boulevard Association, was won by Jeff Bradley, of Davenport, Iowa. (Courtesy of Oscar Wastyn Archives.)

Four

HISTORIC VENUES

Chicago's bicycling history can be found on the streets and in the parks throughout the city. From bicycle factories converted to present-day apartments and condominiums to velodromes and wide city boulevards, Chicago has a long list of historic venues.

While many of the early factories and stadiums have been torn down, one can still find traces of the past. The Chicago Stadium, International Amphitheatre, the Chicago Coliseum, Western Wheel Works, and Schwinn factory have all met the wrecking ball, but sites like the Northbrook Velodrome and Kenosha Velodrome still host races today. The Sears, Roebuck and Co. distribution facility is gone, but the first Sears Tower (the 14-story administrative building) is still standing.

The city's network of boulevards was the idea of visionary Chicagoans who, in the 1860s, envisioned a network of city parks on the north, west, and south sides linked together by a series of boulevards. The parks and landscaped boulevards offered a respite from the noise and crowds of the surrounding neighborhoods. A city resident could easily ride the boulevards network to and from these wonderfully landscaped parks. Today, some of the factory buildings along West Lake Street in Chicago, or "Bicycle Row" as it was once known, are still standing and have been repurposed as condominium and apartment developments. The Lake Street Lofts Building on Lake Street was the first home of Arnold, Schwinn & Company. Cobbler's Square Lofts on Wells Street is the former Western Wheel Works factory.

While many historic venues are gone, some still survive to this day, a reminder of Chicago's cycling past.

COLISEUM-CHICAGO

The Chicago Coliseum was located at Fifteenth Street and Wabash Avenue on the near south side. This was the third of three arenas to be called the Chicago Coliseum. (Courtesy of Oscar Wastyn Archives.)

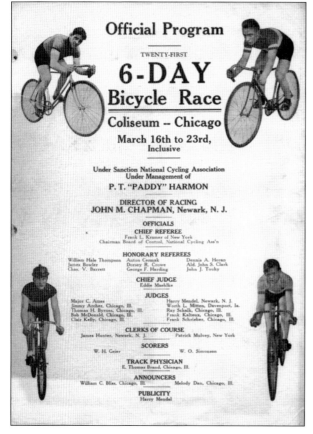

Seen here is the official program cover from a 6-day race at the Chicago Coliseum. (Courtesy of Oscar Wastyn Archives.)

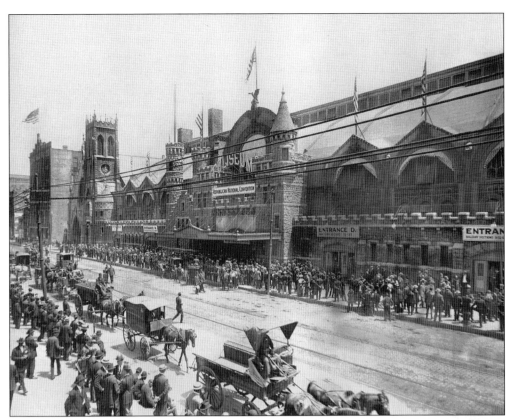

The Chicago Coliseum hosted 6-day races in the 1920s, 1930s, and 1940s. American riders such as Bill Jacoby, Ed Carfagnini, Freddie Spencer, and Bobby Walthour Jr. all made names for themselves racing at venues such as the Chicago Coliseum and Madison Square Garden in New York City. The coliseum fell into disrepair and was eventually demolished in 1982. (Courtesy of the *Chicago Tribune*.)

Price 15c :: Pay No More

OFFICIAL PROGRAM
Fourth International
SIX-DAY BIKE RACE
Under the Auspices of P. T. HARMON and the
CYCLE RACING ASSOCIATION, Inc., OF NEW YORK
(Sanction of National Cycling Assn.)

October 29th, to Nov. 4th, Inclusive
1922

ERNEST KOCKLER

COLISEUM EXPOSITION BUILDING
Sixteenth Street and Wabash Avenue
Chicago

P. T. HARMON, Publisher

32

The official program cover from the 6-day race in 1922 at the Chicago Coliseum is seen here. (Courtesy of Oscar Wastyn Archives.)

Seen here is a 1927 official program cover for a 6-day race. (Courtesy of Oscar Wastyn Archives.)

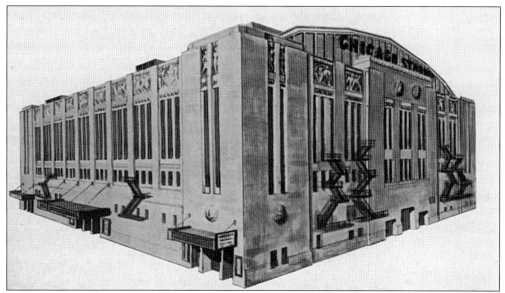

The Chicago Stadium, built in 1929, hosted 6-day races in the late 1920s, 1930s, and 1940s. (Courtesy of Oscar Wastyn Archives.)

Pictured here is the cover photograph of the *Chicago Stadium Review* in 1930. (Courtesy of Oscar Wastyn Archives.)

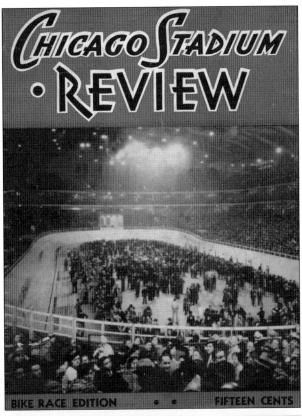

A capacity crowd at the Chicago Stadium waits for the start of a Chicago Blackhawks game in 1930. (Courtesy of Oscar Wastyn Archives.)

The International Amphitheatre was located on the city's west side at Halsted and Forty-Second Streets. The amphitheater, adjacent to the Union Stock Yards, stood from 1934 to 1999. It hosted 6-day races in the 1930s, 1940s, and even the late 1950s. (Courtesy of Oscar Wastyn Archives.)

A cover page from a 6-day race program at the International Amphitheatre is pictured here. The race took place from March 21 to March 27, 1935. (Courtesy of Oscar Wastyn Archives.)

Shewbridge Stadium held track cycling events in the late 1950s hosted by the Chicago Bi-Cycling Association. Shewbridge Stadium was located at 7400 South Morgan Street. There were afternoon races starting at 2:00 p.m. and evening races starting at 8:00 p.m. (Courtesy of Oscar Wastyn Archives.)

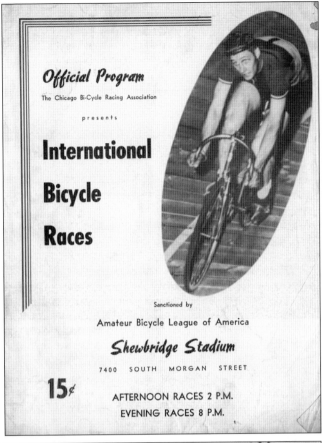

Official Program
The Chicago Bi-Cycle Racing Association

presents

International

Bicycle

Races

Sanctioned by

Amateur Bicycle League of America

Shewbridge Stadium

7400   SOUTH   MORGAN   STREET

15¢   AFTERNOON RACES 2 P.M.
EVENING RACES 8 P.M.

The Humboldt Park Velodrome was built in 1928. From 1928 to 1932, the track surface was cement. In 1932, a wooden track was built over the concrete surface. Wednesday night races were regular fixtures at the track. It hosted outdoor 6-day races in 1935 and 1936. (Courtesy of Oscar Wastyn Archives.)

A group of racers relaxes for a photograph on the track in the early 1940s, Track racing flourished for over a decade until World War II. The wooden track was expensive to maintain, and the construction materials used on the track were difficult to come by due to war rationing. The track began to deteriorate, and it burned in 1946. The remaining portion of the track was demolished in early 1962. (Courtesy of Oscar Wastyn Archives.)

A wooden track is shown being built over the existing concrete surface at the Humboldt Park Velodrome in 1934. This was a Works Progress Administration (WPA) project. The WPA helped idle workers carry out Depression-era public works projects. (Courtesy of Oscar Wastyn Archives.)

The temporary cycling track at Gately Park was located on 103rd Street on the south side of the city. During the 1959 Pan American Games, the United States won a gold medal in the Team Pursuit Men (4000m, track). Jack Disney won silver at the Match Sprint Men (1000m, track), and David Staub won a silver in the Time Trial Men (1000m). (Courtesy of Oscar Wastyn Archives.)

The 1948 US National Track Championships were held at the Kenosha Velodrome. Ted Smith, of Buffalo, New York, won the race. Smith was the Amateur Bicycling League of America Champion (the youngest champion to date) in 1945, 1947, and 1948. He was a member of the 1948 Olympic team. He raced in Belgium in 1950 as a professional, becoming the first US rider to compete in the World's Pro Road Race Championships. (Courtesy of Bob Wischer.)

Watching track racing on "the hill," spectators could see races free of charge on any day or night of racing. While located across the border in Kenosha, Wisconsin, the Kenosha Velodrome has been a draw for Chicago-area track racers for decades. (Courtesy of Oscar Wastyn Archives.)

Two riders approach the finish at a race in the 1950s at the Kenosha Velodrome. During a sprint to the finish line, racers can approach 40–45 miles per hour. (Courtesy of Oscar Wastyn Archives.)

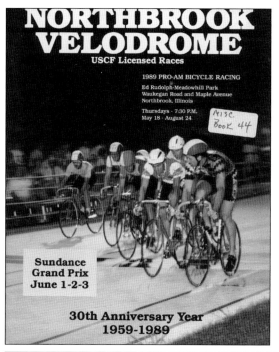

The Ed Rudolph Velodrome (commonly known as the Northbrook Velodrome) is located in Northbrook, Illinois. It hosts track cycling events during the spring and summer months. The grassy infield is used for youth and adult soccer games. Constructed in 1960, it is owned by the Northbrook Park District. Thursday night races are a tradition in the Chicago track community. Originally, the velodrome had a dirt-paved track. The original track was built by Ed Rudolph and employees of his landscaping company. It was later upgraded with an asphalt surface. (Courtesy of Oscar Wastyn Archives.)

A program cover from the 1966 racing season at the Northbrook Velodrome is shown here. Thursday night races are a tradition at the track and continue today—55-plus years after the track opened in 1960. (Courtesy of Oscar Wastyn Archives.)

Arnold, Schwinn & Company original factory at Peoria and Lake Streets, Chicago

The former Arnold, Schwinn & Company headquarters is pictured here. In the 1900s, more than 30 bicycle manufactures were located along Chicago's West Lake Street, commonly known as "Bicycle Row." Schwinn moved to a new, larger factory on North Kildare Avenue in 1901. (Courtesy of Oscar Wastyn Archives.)

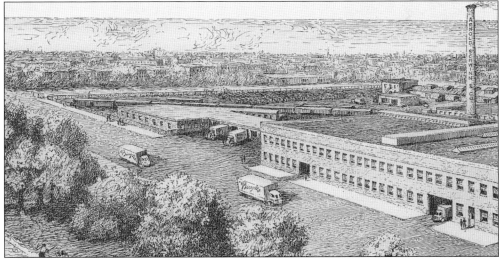

The Schwinn factory was located at 1718 North Kildare. As the company grew, it need more space than the Lake Street headquarters could provide. In 1901, it relocated to the Kildare Avenue facility and stayed there until 1983, when most of the production had shifted to the southern United States and overseas. (Courtesy of Oscar Wastyn Archives.)

The Monarch Cycle Manufacturing Company factory was located at North Halsted and Lake Streets. Founded by John Kiser in 1892, Monarch quickly became one of the country's largest bicycle manufacturers during the 1890s. In 1899, John Kiser sold the Monarch Cycle Manufacturing Company to a "bicycle trust"—just before the sales crashed due to the rise of the automobile. (Courtesy of Oscar Wastyn Archives.)

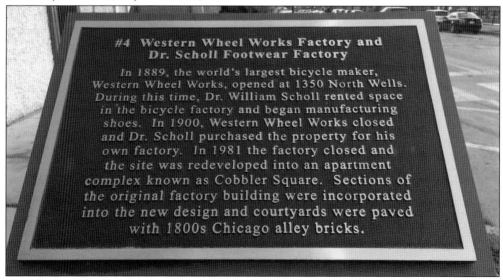

The Western Wheel Works factory was located at Wells and Schiller Streets. For several years, it was the largest bike factory in the world. Western Wheel Works manufactured the popular Crescent, Blackhawk, and Rob Roy bicycles. It went out of business in 1900, and its building was purchased by Dr. William Scholl, owner of the shoe and foot-care company known as Dr. Scholl's.

Western Wheel Works Factory, Chicago, U.S.A.

The Western Wheel Works factory was purchased by Dr. William Scholl. Dr. Scholl's was located in the building until 1981. It was then converted to a residential condominium complex called Cobbler's Square. (Courtesy of Oscar Wastyn Archives.)

The original Kozy's Bicycle Store was located on Milwaukee Avenue. Kozy's has been family owned since 1944. (Courtesy of Kozy's Bicycles.)

On the Route Bicycles' original location was on the northwest corner of Belmont and Southport Avenues in 1971. Columbian cyclist Armando Gallo founded Bicicletaria La Ruta in the Lakeview neighborhood. Gallo later adopted the roughly translated On the Route store name. (Courtesy of On the Route.)

In 1936, Oscar Wastyn Cycles was located at 2221 North Milwaukee Avenue. (Courtesy of Oscar Wastyn Archives.)

Evo Passaglia (left), Pierre Devise (center), and Bill Jacoby (right) line up at the start of a criterium race at Sherman Park. The park has been the site of cycling races for over a century. (Courtesy of Oscar Wastyn Archives.)

Mountain biking is popular at the Palos Forest Preserve. The Chicago Area Mountain Bikers Association (CAMBr) works with the Cook County Forest Preserve District to maintain an extensive network of mountain bike trails. (Courtesy of CAMBr.)

Founded in 1893, Sears, Roebuck and Co. was the country's largest mail-order company by 1900. In 1904, it purchased 41 acres on Chicago's west side for its corporate complex. The massive facility opened in 1906. (Courtesy of the North Homan Foundation.)

From left to right, Frank Brilando, Keith Kingbay, Al Cress, and Spike Shannon ride a Schwinn Town and Country outside the Schwinn factory at 1718 North Kildare Avenue in Chicago in the late 1960s. (Courtesy of Oscar Wastyn Archives.)

Five

CYCLING PERSONALITIES

Strong, colorful personalities dominated the sport and the business of cycling. People like Ignaz Schwinn, Marshall "Major" Taylor, Carl Stockholm, Annie Londonderry, and May Theirgard Watts, just to name a few, all contributed to make Chicago one of the best bicycling cities in the world.

In the late 19th century, entrepreneurs flocked to Chicago to start bicycle companies. Chicago was just a couple of decades removed from the Great Chicago Fire of 1871, and it was a growing transportation and industrial center.

The national rail network provided the means to get finished products to market, and a skilled workforce made Chicago a great location for entrepreneurs of the era. The presence of numerous bicycle manufacturers drew cyclists from throughout the country. A.A. Zimmerman won the first International Cycling Association championship in 1893 at the World's Columbian Exposition. Major Taylor set the one-mile track cycling championship in 1899 at Chicago's Garfield Park Velodrome. Carl Stockholm was successful on the velodrome and in Chicago business. Phyllis Harmon, known as "The Grand Dame of Bicycling," led the resurgence of the League of American Bicyclists, and Ignaz Schwinn founded one of the great American industrial companies, Arnold, Schwinn & Company, in Chicago in 1895.

Ignaz Schwinn was born in Hardheim, Germany, in 1860. He moved to the United States in 1891, and in October 1895, he incorporated Arnold, Schwinn & Company. By the end of the decade, Schwinn was the leader in technology and innovation. After his death in 1948, his son Frank assumed leadership of the company. (Courtesy of Oscar Wastyn Archives.)

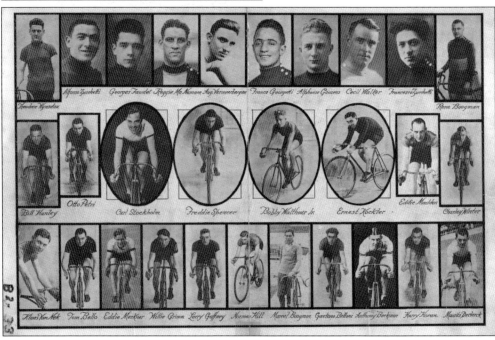

Pictured here are cycling stars of the 1920s and 1930s. Riders such as Carl Stockholn, Eddie Spencer, Bobby Walthour Jr., and Ernest Kockler were featured racers at 6-day races at the Chicago Coliseum and the Chicago Stadium. (Courtesy of Oscar Wastyn Archives.)

Carter Harrison Jr. served as mayor of Chicago from 1897 to 1905 and again from 1911 to 1915. He was the son of Carter Harrison Sr., who served as mayor from 1879 to 1887 and in 1893. During the younger Harrison's first campaign for mayor, he produced posters with the slogan "Not a Champion Cyclist, but the Cyclists Champion." Harrison believed that support from the bicycle community contributed to his victory over four other challengers in the 1897 race. (Courtesy of Oscar Wastyn Archives.)

Christian Vande Velde grew up in suburban Lemont. He raced for the United States Postal Service pro racing team, including several appearances in the Tour de France. He is the son of John Vande Velde. Christian is pictured at Oscar Wastyn Cycles with a Schwinn Paramount racing bike. (Courtesy of Oscar Wastyn Archives.)

Mayor Richard M. Daley (left) and Randy Neufeld, of the Chicago Bicycle Federation (now Active Transportation Alliance), ride a tandem bike in Daley Plaza. (Courtesy of Active Transportation Alliance.)

In 1910, Belgian bicycle builder Emil Wasytn emigrated to the United States. He opened a bicycle shop on Fullerton Avenue and began a family dynasty that would span more than a century. In 1937, he designed and built the first Schwinn Paramount. He is pictured here with his wife, Louise. (Courtesy of Oscar Wastyn Archives.)

Oscar Wastyn Sr. was one of Schwinn's top dealers and praised the company for its commitment to quality and safety. Wastyn built the Wastyn Special and Wastyn Custom bikes along with the Schwinn Paramount line. He was chief mechanic for over twenty 6-day races. He built custom frames for cycling Hall of Famers Jim Rossi, John Vande Velde, and Cecil Yates and served as an official at both the Northbrook and Kenosha Velodromes. (Courtesy of Oscar Wastyn Archives.)

"Bicycle Racing Stars of the Nineteenth Century" held their first 1st reunion on September 5, 1941. It was organized by Oscar Wastyn Sr. at the Sportsmans Golf Course. (Courtesy of Oscar Wastyn Archives.)

The 10th annual reunion of bicycle racing stars of the 19th century was held in September 1950. (Courtesy of Oscar Wastyn Archives.)

The 22nd annual reunion of bicycle racing stars of the 19th century was held in October 1961 at the Wagon Wheel Grill in Chicago. (Courtesy of Oscar Wastyn Archives.)

Oscar Wastyn Jr. is pictured officiating a track race at the Northbrook Velodrome. Wastyn is the son of Oscar Wastyn Sr. Among his many accomplishments are former board member of the US Bicycling Hall of Fame, former president of the Schwinn Lakeshore Wheelmen, and former vice president of the Northbrook Cycling Committee. (Courtesy of Oscar Wastyn Archives.)

Oscar Wastyn Jr. stands with a Schwinn Paramount at his store, Oscar Wastyn Cycles, on Fullerton Avenue in Chicago. Wastyn has remarkable knowledge of American cycling history and maintains extensive archives. (Courtesy of Oscar Wastyn Archives.)

Carl Stockholm excelled in many areas. After his successful Olympic and professional career, Stockholm served in World War II as senior officer in the South Pacific fleet. In 1954, Quaker Oats produced a trading card recalling his cycling career. He promoted ski-jumping events staged on an artificial hill at Soldier Field and was chairman of the 1959 Pan American Games, held in Chicago. He was also cochairman of the committee that rescued the German U-505 sub and brought it to Chicago to become a permanent museum exhibit. Stockholm also owned and managed farms in Dane County, Wisconsin, and Lake County, Illinois, as well as orange groves in Florida. He was the director and past president of the Garfield Business Men's Association and the past president of the Merchandise Mart Retailers Association. He owned and managed Carl Stockholm Cleaners from 1927 to 1974. Stockholm died in 1996. (Courtesy of Oscar Wastyn Archives.)

Dr. Paul Dudley White and Mayor Richard J. Daley (at front handlebars) are riding a tandem bike to help open a bicycle path on Ogden Avenue in Chicago in 1956. White was one of the nation's leading cardiologists and an avid promoter of exercise and healthy lifestyles. Pres. Lyndon Johnson presented White the Presidential Medal of Freedom for his work in medicine in September 1964. Mayor Richard J. Daley's son, Mayor Richard M. Daley, was a huge proponent of bicycling, both for commuters and for recreation. His administration initiated the installation of over 10,000 city-owned bike racks, over 100 miles of new bike lanes, the Divvy program, Bike the Drive, Bike to Work Rally, and the formation of the Mayor's Bicycle Advisory Council (MBAC) in order to encourage bicycling in the city. (Courtesy of the City of Chicago.)

May Theirgard Watts, founder of the Illinois Prairie Path, was born in 1893. She worked as a naturalist at the Morton Arboretum in Lisle, Illinois, and retired in 1961. Following retirement, she wrote a column in the *Chicago Tribune* and had an educational horticultural program on public television. Her public education efforts led to the promotion of what would later become the Illinois Prairie Path. In addition to recognition of her work on the Illinois Prairie Path, May T. Watts Nature Park in Highland Park and the May Watts Elementary School in Naperville are named after her. Watts passed away in 1975. (Courtesy of the Illinois Central College IPP archives.)

Ed Rudolph contributed to the sports of cycling and speed skating in the city of Northbrook. He helped found the Northbrook Skating Club. The Northbrook club has produced numerous Olympians and national and world champions. Rudolph was a commissioner and past president of the Northbrook Park District. He is best known for his work in developing the Olympic cycling track now known as the Ed Rudolph Velodrome. Rudolph helped design and build the velodrome in 1960. The facility features a 382-meter/18-degree banked track for cycling and a grassy infield for soccer games. Rudolph passed away in 2001. (Courtesy of Oscar Wastyn Archives.)

A happy George Garner (above) smiles at the Sacramento Velodrome on July 3, 1948, after winning the top points trophy. A World War II veteran, he opened his first store, named Valley Cyclery, in Van Nuys, California, in 1947. He opened it with the $1,500 he had saved and an additional $1,500 he had borrowed. Garner designed and built his own fixtures for professionally displaying bikes and accessories and prioritized sales and product training for staff. Within a few years, Garner opened four Los Angeles–area stores and became Schwinn's top dealer. Based on Garner's sales model, Schwinn company executives created a sales template called the "total concept store" for other Schwinn dealers to implement. In 1965, Schwinn asked Garner to open a store in Northbrook, Illinois (below). Garner was Schwinn's No. 1 dealer for 17 years in a row, and at his peak, sold 10,000 bikes per year. He eventually opened three more stores in the Chicagoland area and continued to operate five in California. Garner passed away in October 2016. (Both, courtesy of George Garner family.)

Stan Day helped found the SRAM Corporation in 1987. SRAM is an acronym for the founders—Scott, Ray, and Sam Day. As a young start-up company, SRAM introduced the Grip Shift (or twist shift) gear-change method to the road bike market in 1988. The Grip Shift technology helped revolutionize the bicycle component market. (Courtesy of the SRAM Corporation.)

Randy Neufeld began his career as a cycling advocate at the Active Transportation Alliance, formally known as the Chicagoland Bicycle Federation. He began as the group's executive director in 1987 and then served as chief strategy officer from 2004 through 2009. Neufeld currently works as the director of the SRAM Cycling Fund. He played a major role in the development of Big Marsh Park, the new eco-recreation park located on Chicago's southeast side. (Courtesy of the SRAM Corporation.)

John Vande Velde competed for the United States at the 1968 and 1972 Olympics on the track, riding team pursuit both years and individual pursuit in 1972. Vande Velde also rode at the 1971 Pan American Games, winning a bronze medal in the team pursuit. After the 1972 Olympics, Vande Velde turned professional and was one of the first American riders to race professionally in Europe. Vande Velde has a small role in the movie *Breaking Away*, in which he plays one of the members of the Cinzano team. He later went into sports marketing and helped stage and manage cycling races. He is also the father of former pro cyclist Christian Vande Velde. (Courtesy of Oscar Wastyn Archives.)

Jim Rossi, of Chicago, Illinois, competed in the Meter Heat Men (4000m) at Northbrook Velodrome. Here, Rossi is riding a Schwinn Paramount. He competed at the 1956 and 1960 Summer Olympics. He was the Senior Men's National Omnium champion from 1959 to 1963. Rossi served as president of the Northbrook Cycle Committee from 1974 to 1977 and again in 1980. He was inducted into the US Bicycling Hall of Fame in 1992. Rossi passed away in 2005. (Courtesy of Oscar Wastyn Archives.)

Oscar Wastyn Sr. works on a racing bike during practice at the Chicago Coliseum. Note the steep angle of the wooden track. (Courtesy of Oscar Wastyn Archives.)

Marshall "Major" Taylor won the world one-mile (1.6 km) track cycling championship in 1899 after setting numerous world records and overcoming racial discrimination. Taylor was the first African American cyclist to achieve the level of world champion. (Courtesy of Oscar Wastyn Archives.)

Major Taylor died on June 21, 1932, at age of 53, in the charity ward of Cook County Hospital. He died a pauper due to bad investments, persistent illness, and the Depression. In 1948, a group of former professional bike racers, with money donated by Schwinn Bicycle Co. president Frank W. Schwinn, organized the exhumation and relocation of Taylor's remains to a more prominent part of Mount Glenwood Cemetery near Chicago. (Courtesy of Oscar Wastyn Archives.)

Erwin Pesak poses with some of his many trophies in the early 1940s. (Photograph by Toivo Kaitila, courtesy of Oscar Wastyn Archives.)

Many of those same trophies are on display today at Oscar Wastyn Cycles. (Courtesy of Oscar Wastyn Archives.)

National Bike Dealer Association president Stanley Kozy and son Ron Kozy are pictured at the 1956 Chicago National Bike Convention. (Courtesy of the Kozy family.)

Frank Brilando of Chicago, Ill.
Winner 1949 50-mile Tour of Somerville N.J.
Third place in 1948 Nationals at Kenosha, Wisc.
Member of 1948 U.S. Olympic Cycling Team to London

Frank Brilando was a member of the 1948 and 1952 US Olympic teams. Brilando joined Schwinn as an engineer in the early 1950s. He went on to head Schwinn's engineering department from the 1960s to the 1980s. (Courtesy of Oscar Wastyn Archives.)

During the 1960s, Phyllis Harmon helped to resurrect the League of American Wheelmen, the oldest bicycling organization in the United States. During her many years with the organization, she served in various positions, including publisher of the *L.A.W. Bulletin* (now the *League of American Bicyclists* magazine). Harmon also formed the Wheeling Wheelmen in 1970. In 2014, she was honored with the dedication of the Phyllis Harmon Trail in Wheeling, Illinois. Known as "The Grand Dame of Bicycling," she was inducted into the US Bicycling Hall of Fame in 2009. Harmon passed away in 2016 at 99 years of age. (Courtesy of the US Bicycling Hall of Fame.)

Six

RAILS TO TRAILS

The Chicago area has an extensive network of rails to trails projects. Rails to trails are abandoned railroad right-of-ways that have been converted into biking, hiking, and walking trails. Currently, Illinois has 78 rails to trails, totaling 909 miles of trails. Another 19 projects are in development, totaling an additional 189 miles of trails statewide. The Chicago area is fortunate enough to have many of these rails to trails projects. Forward-thinking community members and political leaders have worked to convert abandoned right-of-ways to parkland and greenways for public use.

The Illinois Prairie Path runs through Chicago's western suburbs and was North America's first successful rails to trails projects; it became a template for future rails to trails and helped launch hundreds of other projects. Over the last few decades, Chicago has added the Skokie Valley Trail, Sauganash Trail, Major Taylor Trail, and, most recently, the Bloomingdale Trail.

In addition, the Chicago area boasts many other recreational trails, such as the Des Plaines River Trail, the Chicago Lakefront Trail, Cal-Sag Trail, and the Big Marsh Park. All contribute to the regional network of trails and greenways that connect communities and provide healthy opportunities for residents.

May Thielgaard Watts was the founder of the Illinois Prairie Path (IPP). In a letter to the editor of the *Chicago Tribune* in 1963, Watts introduces the concept of a regional trail through DuPage County. In the letter, she calls for the Chicago Aurora & Elgin (CA&E) Railroad right-of-way to be preserved and not given over to developers. (Courtesy of North Central College IPP archives.)

The North Avenue overpass above the CA&E right-of-way is seen here. This photograph was taken by S.S. Holmes III of his cousin Eleanor in 1966. (Courtesy of North Central College IPP archives.)

Volunteers on the old CA&E train bridge (now called Volunteer Bridge) watch as the new Front Street section is lowered into place in late October 1983. (Courtesy of North Central College IPP archives.)

Pictured is the ribbon cutting at the main stem section on First Avenue in Maywood on September 20, 1998. Jean Mooring (original IPP board member) is at right taking pictures. In August 2006, a new pedestrian bridge was built over the Des Plaines River, connecting Maywood and Forest Park. This extension allows the main stem of the Illinois Prairie Path to terminate farther east, at the Forest Park CTA station. (Courtesy of North Central College IPP archives.)

An eastbound CA&E train, No. 418, arrives from the Villa Park station on June 23, 1953. CA&E abruptly ended service on July 3, 1957. Freight service continued for two more years, until that ended on June 10, 1959. Today, the once thriving railroad is just a distant memory. (Courtesy of North Central College IPP archives.)

Shown here is a view of Lincoln Marsh Natural Area in Wheaton. In 1979, the Wheaton Park District and several other local and state agencies began purchasing parcels of land that form the core of Lincoln Marsh. Today, the natural area features more than 150 acres of rare wetlands, woodlands, and prairie in the middle of west suburban Wheaton. (Courtesy of North Central College IPP archives.)

The front page of the first newsletter for what would become Illinois Prairie Path is seen here in 1963. The cover includes May Thielgaard Watts's letter to the editor of the *Chicago Tribune*. (Courtesy of North Central College IPP archives.)

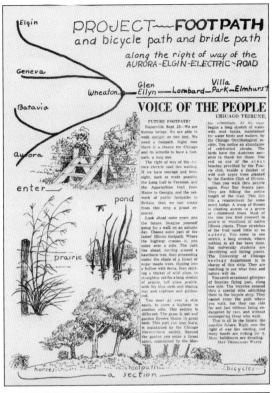

IPP board member Betty Nemec volunteers at the IPP booth at the World Flower and Garden Show at McCormick Place in Chicago in the early 1970s. (Courtesy of North Central College IPP archives.)

Volunteers are stretching the fence on Volunteer Bridge in Wheaton, Illinois, in 1983. (Courtesy of North Central College IPP archives.)

Cyclists enjoy a Saturday afternoon on the path in 1973. (Courtesy of North Central College IPP archives.)

The Major Taylor Trail is a six-mile rails to trails bike path stretching though Chicago's south side and the village of Riverdale. Created in the late 1990s from an old rail line, the Major Taylor Trail serves as a link between the Dan Ryan Woods in Chicago and the Whistler Woods in Riverdale. (Courtesy of the Friends of the Major Taylor Trail.)

Cyclists prepare to leave from the Major Taylor mural, located along the path at 111th Street. The Chicago & Great Eastern Railroad right-of-way was finally abandoned in the 1980s after being in operation since 1865. A new trail opened on June 2, 2007, after years of discussion and planning. The advocacy group, Friends of the Major Taylor Trail, worked to make the trail a reality and today helps to maintain and improve the trail through trail workdays, Earth Day celebrations, and public awareness rides. (Courtesy of the Friends of the Major Taylor Trail.)

The Green Bay Trail runs on the former Chicago North Shore & Milwaukee right-of-way for nine miles, from Winnetka to Highland Park. It runs parallel to the Metra North commuter railroad line. The Chicago North Shore & Milwaukee Railroad abandoned the right-of-way in 1955 and it was leased to the Green Bay Trail Committee for development. In 2014, a crossover trail was constructed to connect with the North Branch Trail in Glencoe. (Courtesy of the Friends of the Green Bay Trail.)

The Fox River Trail begins in Algonquin, at the Kane/McHenry county line, and runs south 38 miles to Oswego in Kendall County. The trail crosses the Fox River in several places. Between Batavia and North Aurora, the trail splits and runs on both sides of the river. Some of the Fox River Trail is built on the former right-of-way of the Aurora, Elgin & Fox River Electric (AE&FRE) interurban railroad and the Chicago & North Western (C&NW) Railroad, but some was constructed specifically as a recreational path. The section of the Fox River Trail connecting the McHenry County Prairie Trail in Algonquin and the Illinois Prairie Path in Elgin is part of the Grand Illinois Trail, linking over 500 miles of trails together throughout Illinois. (Courtesy of the Friends of the Fox River Trail.)

The Bloomingdale Trail is the focus of a park and trail network known as the "606." The network's name is taken from the city's area code, 606. This symbolizes the bringing together of the many diverse neighborhoods along the trail. (Courtesy of the Friends of the Bloomingdale Trail.)

Nature reclaimed the space following the closure of the rail line. In 1997, the Daley Administration and surrounding neighborhood groups first introduced the plan for converting the Bloomingdale Line into a greenway. It formally proposed the idea in the Logan Square Open Space Plan in 2002. This plan proposed a linear park or greenway with access ramps every few blocks apart. At the east end, a trailhead would be created at the Chicago River. (Courtesy of the Friends of the Bloomingdale Trail.)

The Des Plaines River Trail runs north-south along the Des Plaines River through Lake and Cook Counties. The more than 56-mile trail connects numerous forest preserves, parks, and suburban communities between Russell, Illinois, and Melrose Park, Illinois. The Des Plaines River trailhead is at North Avenue in Melrose Park, in the Jerome Huppert Woods, which takes a rider all the way to Lake Cook Road and the entrance to Lake County. The total mileage in Cook County is about 17 miles. (Courtesy of the Forest Preserve District of Cook County.)

The Sauganash Trail officially opened on June 21, 2008, in the Sauganash community, located on Chicago's northwest side. The path is approximately one mile long and runs from Bryn Mawr Avenue to Devon Avenue, where it connects with the Lincolnwood Valley Trail.

The Great Western Trail runs along the Chicago Great Western Rail Corridor through DuPage and Kane Counties in west suburban Chicago. The western portion runs 18 miles between St. Charles in Kane County and Sycamore in DeKalb County and was converted to a recreational trail after the line was abandoned in 1977. The eastern portion of the trail runs 12 miles between Elmhurst and West Chicago. The eastern part of the trail ends in Elmhurst at the restored Chicago Great Western (CGW) Railroad depot. In 1995, the trail was extended to connect with the Illinois Prairie Path. Using this intersection, riders can access the 62-mile Illinois Prairie Path. (Courtesy of the Friends of the Great Western Trail.)

The North Shore Bike Path runs between Lake Bluff and Mundelein, paralleling State Route 176 for the path's entire length. At its eastern end, the North Shore Bike Path connects to the Robert McClory Bike Path at Sheridan Road and Scranton Avenue. Just east of Libertyville, the North Shore Bike Path links to the north-south running Des Plaines River Trail. (Courtesy of the Friends of the North Shore Bike Path.)

A CGW freight train is passing the railroad depot in Elmhurst in 1962. The Chicago Great Western Railroad Depot was acquired by the Elmhurst Park District from the Chicago & North Western Railroad in 1971. It was renovated by the park district in 1975 and dedicated on July 4, 1976. Today, it is used for children's and general recreation programs. (Courtesy of the Friends of the Great Western Trail.)

Two former railroad right-of-ways, the Chicago Great Western and Chicago, Aurora & Elgin, run parallel through Elmhurst. The Great Western Prairie lies between the two and is the only place in the western suburbs with preserved native prairie. The land is maintained by the Elmhurst Park District. The right-of-way of the Chicago, Aurora & Elgin is now occupied by the Illinois Prairie Path.

Seven

TODAY AND BEYOND

Since the beginning of the bicycle industry in the 1890s, Chicago has been one of the premier cycling locations in the country. Today, that it is even more apparent. In 2016, *Bicycling* magazine named Chicago the most bike-friendly city in the United States. This award was the culmination of years of work by the City of Chicago, the Chicago-based Active Transportation Alliance, and local cycling groups, all devoted to improving bicycling in Chicago.

Strong, pro-bicycling mayors such as Carter H. Harrison II, Richard J. Daley, Richard M. Daley, and Rahm Emmanuel have all made lasting contributions to bicycling in Chicago. In 2013, the Divvy bike-sharing system began operations with 750 bike and 75 stations. The program has been a huge hit with Chicago residents and today has over 580 stations. The city continues to cosponsor events such as Bike the Drive, Bike to Work Week, Boulevard Lakefront Tour, Bike Chicago, and the LATE Ride, all designed to promote bicycling as a recreational pastime and a commuting alternative.

Over the last few years, the city has created over 100 miles of dedicated bike lanes, 165 miles of signed bike lanes, and 10,000 bike racks. The McDonald's Cycle Center in Millennium Park and the additions of the Bloomingdale Trail (also known as the 606) on the north side and Big Marsh Park on the south side have added new recreational opportunities for urban cyclists.

Chicago is fortunate to have a number of advocacy groups and clubs that help to promote a pro-cycling agenda throughout the city and suburbs. The Active Transportation Alliance, Friends of the Parks, Evanston Bike Club, Chicago Cycling Club, Slow Roll Chicago, West Town Bikes, and others all contribute to improving the Chicago cycling community.

Ancien Cycles and Cafe, located at 1558 East Fifty-Third Street in the Hyde Park neighborhood, is a unique hospitality cycle lounge featuring bikes, coffee, and food. Bikes and beer/coffee is a tradition, and Chicago has several excellent combination bike stores and coffee shops. (Courtesy of Ancien Cycles and Cafe.)

Village Cycle Center is the nation's largest Trek Bikes dealer and features an inventory of over 10,000 bikes in stock. The store is located across the street from the former Western Wheel Works factory, which is now the Cobbler Square condominium building.

Heritage Bicycles is located at 2959 North Lincoln Avenue in Chicago. The store, one of three locations in the city, is a combination neighborhood coffee shop and bicycle store. Heritage Bicycles produces American-made custom bikes for commuters and serious racers. (Courtesy of Heritage Bicycles.)

Spokes, located in suburban Wheaton and Naperville, hosts popular road and mountain bike group rides several days each week throughout the western suburbs. (Courtesy of Raouf Radi.)

The McDonald's Cycle Center is an indoor/outdoor bike station located in Chicago's Millennium Park. The bike station serves commuters and recreational riders and features lockers, showers, a snack bar, bike repair, bike rental, and over 300 bicycle parking spaces. The center opened in July 2004. Cyclists, along with urban planners and environmentalists, see the McDonald's Cycle Center as a huge success story in urban planning and transit-oriented development. It cost $3.2 million to build. Federal grants from the Federal Highway Administration and the Federal Transit Administration, along with City of Chicago money, paid for the project.

The new SRAM corporate headquarters is located at 1000 West Fulton Street in Chicago. The new offices have 72,000 square feet of bicycle-themed features, including a bike path that winds around the work floor. The former Fulton Cold Storage Building was transformed from an empty meatpacking and food distribution structure into a technology hub. Google occupies the other floors in the building. (Courtesy of the SRAM Corporation.)

World Bicycle Relief is an international, nonprofit organization based in Chicago that specializes in bicycle distribution programs to aid poverty relief in developing countries around the world. It has distributed more than 275,000 bicycles and trained more than 1,000 bicycle mechanics in the developing world. World Bicycle Relief was founded in 2005 by SRAM cofounder and executive vice president F.K. Day. (Courtesy of the SRAM Corporation.)

A hardy recumbent cyclist rides on the Cal-Sag Trial on a chilly spring day in 2015. Approximately 50 percent of the land used for the project was set aside by the Metropolitan Water Reclamation District of Chicago. Federal grants paid for over 80 percent of the trail's construction. (Courtesy of Friends of the Cal-Sag Trail.)

Mayor Rahm Emmanuel rides his bike at the opening of the Bloomingdale Trail (also known as the 606) on June 6, 2016. Emmanuel has been a strong advocate of making Chicago even more bike friendly during his administration. (Courtesy of the Friends of the Bloomingdale Trail.)

The Chicago Lakefront Trail runs 18.5 miles along the Lake Michigan shoreline. In the 1950s, Chicago had a small number of bike paths. Under the leadership of Mayor Richard J. Daley, the city increased the number of bike paths and lanes. By the early 1970s, the city had developed an elaborate network of bikes lanes, including an expanded Lakefront Trail and on-street bike lanes. The trail runs entirely within the city limits. From north to south, it runs through Lincoln Park, Grant Park, Burnham Park, and Jackson Park. (Courtesy of the Chicago Department of Transportation.)

XXX Racing-Athletico racing team is a Chicago-based amateur cycling team. Founded in 1999, it has grown into one of the largest cycling teams in the country. It was awarded the USA Cycling Team of the Year award in 2010, 2013, and 2015. (Courtesy of XXX Racing-Athletico.)

The Intelligensia Cup is the premier pro/amateur cycling series in the Chicagoland area. The series features ten continuous days of racing, including three road races along with seven criterium races. The series is sponsored by Intelligensia Coffee and SRAM.

Cyclo-cross racers sprint out the starting chute at the Caldwell Woods Chicago Cross Cup race in the fall of 2017. The series features 10 different venues during the September–December season. The Chicago Cross Cup was started in 2004 by a group of local cyclo-cross riders from the Chicago area. Today, it is one of the largest cyclo-cross circuits in the United States. Held on Sundays, it attracts 700–800 racers each week. (Courtesy of Scott Rothbarth.)

Steve Buchtel, executive director of Trails for Illinois, surveys the future Big Marsh Park. Buchtel was instrumental in the early days of Park No. 564, as it was originally known. He continues to advocate for the Big Marsh project along with many other existing and future trail projects throughout Illinois. (Courtesy of Friends of Big Marsh.)

A poster promotes Big Marsh Park. The 278-acre park, which opened on November 6, 2016, is located on Chicago's southeast side and is slightly smaller than Chicago's famous Grant Park. The park, built on environmentally neglected and misused land, features wetlands, walking trails, cyclo-cross trails, and a BMX park. It is Chicago's first eco-recreation park. (Courtesy of Friends of Big Marsh.)

Chicago mayor Rahm Emmanuel speaks at the opening of Big Marsh Park on November 6, 2016. The opening ceremony marked the end of years of discussion, planning, and construction to transform the neglected land into a huge recreational asset for southeast-side residents. (Courtesy of Friends of Big Marsh.)

In 2007, Mayor Daley visited Paris, France, where he tested the Velib bicycle-sharing program. Upon returning home, he set out a plan to develop a similar system in Chicago. The city then requested proposals from private sector partners to create a similar program in Chicago. Divvy is the popular bicycle-sharing program located throughout the city. It currently operates over 5,800 bicycles at 580 stations. Divvy officially began operations on June 28, 2013, with 750 bikes and 75 stations. The Divvy program is operated by the Motivate Corporation for the Chicago Department of Transportation. (Courtesy of the Chicago Department of Transportation.)

Chicago Bike Week, sponsored by the Active Transportation Alliance, is a weeklong celebration of cycling. The series of events and rallies help cyclists celebrate and learn more about bike riding in Chicago. The week culminates with a Friday morning Bike to Work Rally held at Daley Plaza. (Courtesy of Active Transportation Alliance.)

The Active Transportation Alliance is a nonprofit advocacy group that works to improve conditions and infrastructure for cyclists in Chicago. The alliance host events such as Bike to Work Week, Winter Bike Challenge, and Bike the Drive. All the events are designed to promote riding and raise money for the alliance's programs. (Courtesy of Active Transportation Alliance.)

Sven Nys (left) and Sven Vanthourenhout (center), both former world cyclo-cross champions, are pictured with the author of *Cycling in Chicago* at the XXX Racing Cyclocross Clinic held in September 2016 at Caldwell Woods on the northwest side of Chicago. The "Svens" led a one-day cyclo-cross clinic benefitting the Pieter Ombregt Scholarship Fund. Nys and Vanthourenhout are two of the greatest names in cyclo-cross history. They have won a combined five world championships, 11 world championship medals, and 24 Belgian National Championships. (Courtesy of XXX Racing-Athletico.)

The Evanston Bicycle Club (EBC) was formed in 1971 with 30 members. Today, it has grown to over 500 members. The EBC has been the organizer of the North Shore Century ride since 1984. Approximately 100 club volunteers help to produce the ride each fall. Over 2,000 riders take part in the event, which travels through the northern suburbs and up to Kenosha. The net proceeds from the North Shore Century are donated to not-for-profit organizations that promote biking and bike safety. (Courtesy of Larry Losoff/Evanston Bicycle Club.)

The Navy Pier Flyover is an elevated bike and pedestrian path extending from the Chicago River Bridge to Jane Addams Park. It is designed to replace one of the most congested portions of the Lakefront Trail. The first phase of the construction began in March 2014. The entire project is scheduled for completion in 2018. (Courtesy of the Chicago Department of Transportation.)

West Town Bikes is a community bicycle learning center located in the Humboldt Park neighborhood. It offers youth programs at the shop on Division Street, along with bicycle mechanic workshops and special events focused towards the community at large. West Town Bikes uses bicycles as a tool to teach its students professionalism, self-reliance, confidence, health and wellness, and positive community involvement. It also hosts group rides, school bike clubs, and after-school programs and apprenticeships. (Courtesy of West Town Bikes.)

Mayor Rahm Emmanuel (center) joins the Major Taylor Cycling Club of Chicago (or MTC3) at the opening of Big Marsh Park. MTC3, based in Chicago's south side, was organized in 2008. The club draws its inspiration from its namesake, Marshall "Major" Taylor, who in 1899 became the first African American world champion in cycling. (Courtesy of Friends of Big Marsh.)

DISCOVER THOUSANDS OF LOCAL HISTORY BOOKS FEATURING MILLIONS OF VINTAGE IMAGES

Arcadia Publishing, the leading local history publisher in the United States, is committed to making history accessible and meaningful through publishing books that celebrate and preserve the heritage of America's people and places.

Find more books like this at
www.arcadiapublishing.com

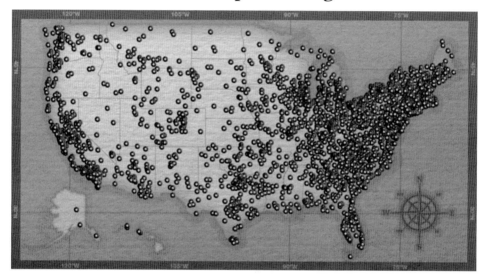

Search for your hometown history, your old stomping grounds, and even your favorite sports team.

Consistent with our mission to preserve history on a local level, this book was printed in South Carolina on American-made paper and manufactured entirely in the United States. Products carrying the accredited Forest Stewardship Council (FSC) label are printed on 100 percent FSC-certified paper.

MADE IN THE USA